Pray & Obey
Ready or Not, Here I Come

SONOVIA WILLIAMS

Dedication

I dedicate this to my husband and my children. My piece of Heaven.

To my husband: Thank you for being you. Thank you for loving me. Thank you for always being there for me even when I wasn't there for myself. Thank you for believing in me. Thank you for encouraging me. You've helped me in more ways than you'll ever know. We've grown together. We've learned together and we've cried together. We've done life together and we will experience the Promised Land together. And because of what God has joined together, now we will celebrate together. Everything that I am is all because of you.

To my children: I give to you a legacy that will break generational curses. A legacy that has allowed me to slay a giant that you and your children and your children's children will never have to face. A legacy that will allow you to birth your purposes and the callings that God has placed down on the inside of you. A legacy that will protect your anointing. A legacy that will allow you to inherit the land and glorify God's kingdom. A legacy that will keep a hedge of protection around you. A legacy that will keep you under the hand of God. A legacy that will change the world for God's glory.

Table of Contents

Note to Self *1*

Business *7*

Depression *15*

Marriage *23*

Spiritually Out of Shape *35*

The Backside of Better *77*

Note to Self

My name is Sonovia Williams. I was born on February 9th, 1980 in Miami, Florida. I am a wife, a mother of 2, and a full time entrepreneur. I find it funny that I started writing this book on Valentine's Day, February 14th, 2020, to profess my love for Christ.

My normal routine consisted of tending to my family, loving my husband and children, and serving my clients. My life seemed pretty simple, but it was just perfect for me. Outside of being a hair stylist and teaching Zumba classes, I also started several businesses that would soon change my life. In my businesses, I had record breaking numbers and the promotions that came along with them. I earned a higher income than I ever imagined. I've traveled places I never thought I would see. I've even connected with people I didn't think would accompany the same room as me. When it came to my business and social media platforms, my name was recognized in lights for my goals and achievements.

Did I mention the part about me being an introvert? I absolutely hate public speaking and large crowds. I loved my little life. It was mine. I worked hard for it. It came with its ups and downs but that's to be expected. I asked the question,

"God, why would You change it?" The answer was that He was preparing me and getting everything in order.

I went from 0 followers to thousands of followers and negative bank accounts to having more than I knew how to spend. I started earning six figures using social media. I went from one house to having two houses. I went from having one car to having one for each day of the work week. I went from having a handful of friends and associates to working and networking with thousands of people. I say this, not to boast, but to show how God works when His hand is on your life.

I was completely broken and in my wilderness when God called me to fulfill my purpose. I started a prayer journal many years ago. Every single day I'd start off my newest entry with *"Dear God…"* I would write down my affirmations, thank Him for my blessings, and ask for the things I needed. I expressed when I was confused and angry about the things that had been going on in my life. God wants us to have a friendship and intimate relationship with Him. Through the good, the bad and the ugly, He wants ALL of us. He even wants the parts of us that we are insecure and vulnerable about. The same parts we hide from the world and even often ourselves.

Getting into alignment with writing this book was tough for me. It meant I had to get uncomfortable. I had to do something I didn't think I was qualified to do. For many years, I've been told that I was supposed to write a book. People would often ask me when my book was coming out. I only have a high school diploma and no college degree. Never in a million years, and barely even now, would I think I would have the title of "Author" next to my name. However, God had a plan.

I had to strip myself of the old me. I had to be broken down. I had to share things with the world that even my own mother didn't know. *Why is it that God insisted on me putting myself out there?* In retrospect, I began to realize that my testimony would be someone else's breakthrough. I discovered that my purpose and God's plan for my life is to break generational curses and bring His people back to His Kingdom. I'm still in awe of His grace and mercy. I'm allowing my heart, and the strength of the Holy Spirit, to guide me as I go.

When I began to write this book, I was under the impression this would take months to complete. This book was not written by flesh but led by the Spirit. With much obedience and tons of faith, I finished this piece exactly 22 days later on March 6th, 2020.

The number 22 is one of the keys to unlocking the mystery of the Bible. The Bible contains 66 books, 3 times 22. There are 22 "Chapter 22's" in the Bible. This is the ONLY chapter in the Bible with the same number of chapters. Psalms 119 is the longest Psalm and sits close to the center of the Bible. This Psalm has

22 verses of 8 lines which start with each of the 22 Hebrew letters. This Psalm is all about praising, respecting and understanding God's word. Psalms 119:105 reads, *"Thy word is a lamp unto my feet, and a light unto my path."*

God created 22 things in the 6 days of creation. A term used by ancient Egyptian priests associated with the number 22 was "A writing from God Himself."

Isaiah 22:22 reads,

> *"And the key of the house of David I will lay on his shoulder; so he shall open, and none shall shut; and he shall shut, and none shall open."*

As you read my story, you will understand the significance of the key and God's word. This is God's miracle. The product is glory but the process is gory. The wilderness is necessary. You can't get to your purpose without going through the wilderness.

Over the next few chapters, you'll see how everything came to pass. You'll see how I became the head and no longer the tail. You'll see how I went from barely enough to more than I could handle. My little private life quickly became a public life, but God had a plan for it all. My hope is that many people will see the goodness of His grace and glory.

If my testimony only touches one person, saves one soul, restores one marriage, brings wholeness into one family or helps someone tap into their destiny, then my job is done. I can only hope sharing what took me years to learn, can give someone a lifetime of hope and strategies. I'm hopeful that it will be applied to many different areas, struggles and storms in your life.

I've always used a hashtag that came to my mind many years ago, #prayandobey. To me, it means to stay prayed up and remain obedient to God's word. Who knew that little idea in my head would later turn into a book for God's glory? *My God! You never cease to amaze me! I can do all things through Christ who gives me strength.*

Exodus 23:20: *"Behold, I send an Angel before thee, to keep thee in the way, and to bring thee into the place which I have prepared."*

Business

After high school, I became a licensed cosmetologist for nearly 20 years. Although I was self-employed, I was robbing Peter to pay Paul. Maybe you can relate to being in this situation at one point in your life. I was absent at times where my presence made the difference. I missed my children's doctor's appointments, football and cheerleading games, and other school functions. The list goes on. I experienced many highs and lows. I dealt with my lights being turned off and cars being repossessed. Life wasn't a walk in the park for me.

We often look for jobs or start businesses based on the potential income. However, if it has purpose attached to it or it will help you towards your purpose, then the end goal will always be worth the journey. When it comes to finding something suitable for your life and needs, there are a few things you should consider:

1. What is my purpose and passion?
2. What makes me hungry?
3. What is my "Why" (Why is this the business for me?)
4. What am I looking to gain?
5. What makes me happy?
6. What makes me feel fulfilled?
7. Will this help me provide for my family?

As my life transitioned, so did my choices and my obedience to God. Being obedient and stepping into God's will changed my life.

In 2013, I started my very first Multi-Level Marketing business or MLM. I worked from home and still worked in the salon. I set my own hours and worked at my own pace. I only started the business to make an extra $200 a month for my family. I was making ends meet but I still felt like I struggling. I wasn't complaining. It was my life and I was COMFORTABLE with it. I had no plans of retirement because I was content with my salon life. I had this idea of growing old in the salon doing press and curls. Fast forward to nearly 3 months in my new business and I already replaced my combined household income. Within 6 months, I was making six figures from my side hustle. I had been doing hair for 20 years and I wasn't making that type of income. With my side hustle, in under a year, I touched money I had never seen before.

I ended up retiring from my salon within the first year of my MLM business. My husband and I were even able to purchase our second home. By that time, my income averaged about $30,000 a month. I was doing this all from a side hustle that I decided to take a leap of faith and start. I traveled many places, changed many lives, and was able to save an additional six figures in my savings account. A major change for someone whose account always stayed in the negative. Struggle was my middle name. At least that's what the enemy wanted me to think. We tend to label ourselves by what we see around us forgetting who we are and whose we are.

A couple of years in, I began to feel unhappy and unfulfilled. Business began to fall apart. I was no longer excited about what I was doing. I began to lose the ranks and titles my team and I achieved. Not long after my income dropped right along with it. I could have easily gone back to the salon but my goal was obedience. I felt like God was telling me it was time for me to move but I still needed a Word from Him. He knows how stubborn His daughter is, but His grace is sufficient. He often would send signs in my dreams or send a Word through someone else. Moments like this is when we must become prepared to see and hear things with our spiritual eyes and ears. It's not in the natural realm, but the spiritual realm.

God will shift things when He is trying to get your attention and get you ready for the next move. I eventually got down on my knees to seek a Word from Him. I soon got the confirmation I was praying for but I sat on it. How often do we strive to be obedient but still question what we're called to do? It usual starts from childhood. For example, our parents tell us what's best for our lives or maybe a situation, but how often did we listen? Many of us would question them. *"How do they know what's right for me?"* Believe it or not, we treat God the same way. He always knows what is best for us. Unfortunately, we oftentimes have to find out by falling on our faces. If only we'd listen when we're told.

Because of my disobedience when God was telling me to make a move, everything began to get worse. I struggled in my business for nearly 6 months before I got my act together. Again, I had gotten COMFORTABLE. I thought I was living my best life. I was traveling and making a more than sufficient income, but God wanted to expose me to more.

I remembered having a dream about being chased by dinosaurs. I did some research and Google says that being chased by a dinosaur in a dream is symbolic of the fear in your life that you're trying to escape. Dreaming of a dinosaur signifies that it's time to put the fear you have behind you and move away from whatever situation that is holding you back. My dreams were affirmed when I received a Word from my Granny. My Granny called and told me God was about to put me back on the bottom only to take me up to the top. She said He wanted to show people He could do it again. He wanted the glory during what I thought was a horrible time in my life.

None of it made any sense to me at the time because I felt like I was already at my best. I had an amazing track record with my business and built my income to six figures. I had retired from my salon and was traveling all around the country. I was even saving more money than I ever had at one time. *How could things possibly get better and why would I want to move?* The Bible says, "…lean not on your own understanding (Proverbs 3:5)." After much debate, I finally realized that, regardless of how I felt or how much I tried to ignore God, my season in that business had finally come to an end. I would be lying if I didn't tell you that in the back of my mind I had questions. *"How could you give me this business, have me help so many people and change their lives, and bless my finances so I could provide for my family, only to have me walk away from it all?"*

In 2018, I started my second home based business. It was in the same field but with different products and a different structure. Everything was on fire. I advanced quickly and was promoted to the top of the company in only 5 months. It would have taken me nearly 5 years to do that with my previous company. What I was previously earning on a monthly basis, I began to earn weekly. *Only God!* I went from starting completely over with no team, to quickly building a massive team. That's how things happen when we follow God and trust where He guides us.

Everyone wanted to know what I was doing and what I had my hands on. They didn't even care that I transitioned from one company and started completely over. They were only interested in how they could possibly do the same. That's what I call favor. When the hand of God is on your life, we must stay obedient to experience all the things He has for us. Even if we stray away, God doesn't change His mind about what He has called us to do.

Then it happened. I started to feel a sense of emptiness yet again. I started thinking to myself, *"God you've got to be kidding me."* I did everything He asked of me and was a good steward over the people He assigned in my life to serve. I began to question why He would even want me to move if things were only going to fall apart again. There was no way I was putting myself in the position to start over again. I'd rather get a job or go back to the salon. How often has God given you a vision or a Word that didn't make sense? How many times has God showed you something that didn't align with what you wanted to do in life? He may have told you to get a job. He may have insisted that you stay at a job that you absolutely despised. He may have wanted you to stay around people that you felt you didn't get along with. Many times we miss the lesson simply because of our own selfish reasons or disbeliefs.

My thoughts were all over the place. *What would my customers think? What would my team think? What would my followers think?* Despite my thoughts, I heard God saying, "What do I think?" I fought Him on this transition because it didn't make any sense to me. However, we're not supposed to see how things will play out. We're just called to be obedient and to trust that He will always know what is best for us.

Instead of leaving like I was supposed to do, I added another business to the list of businesses I currently had. I was doing what God wanted and a little bit of what I wanted too. I could have the best of both worlds, right? Well, at least that's what I thought.

    I started this newest business in 2019 while also doing the business God told me to walk away from. Things started off pretty good. I met some amazing new people. I started networking in new circles and was in a position to change more lives. Although things felt good, God constantly reminded me that I was not doing what He called me to do. Because I was acting out of disobedience, this is the year my depression kicked in. This was something I had never experienced before in my life. I knew others that suffered with it but never in a million years did I think that it could take over my life.

Depression

Depression is feelings of severe dejection; a long and severe recession.

Depression and anxiety can sometimes be hidden. They are silent battles we fight that even those closest to us have no idea that we are fighting. My depression began to surface around the summer of 2018. It lasted nearly 6 months. Most of the time I didn't know if I was coming or going. I struggled because I had no idea how bad it really was. I lost all of my joy, hope, excitement, and creativity. Even worse, it felt like I was losing my faith too. Everything about my life just felt blah. I had no emotions; just darkness and emptiness. It felt as if my entire life was falling apart.

I continued to write in my prayer journal with what little hope I had left but I wasn't using the time to fully seek God. I even stopped going to church and paying my tithes. When we are out of alignment, you can expect for God to shake your world when He wants your attention. We serve a jealous God, and in moments of despair, we give the enemy too much credit by saying the devil is busy. However, even the devil can only do what God allows.

I would stay in the house for days at a time. I didn't want to be around anyone including my own family. I did not want to be a Debbie Downer. I preferred to keep my problems and burdens to myself. I thought it was the right thing to do. I can appreciate those friends that understood when I was really silent. Although they did reach out to check on me from time to time, it still was not enough to fill the void that I felt inside. My husband tried to help but he too could not understand. My mom tried to step in and cheer me up but nothing would shake the empty feeling. It was not until I became fully aware of what I was dealing with, that I learned how to handle and cope with it. It wasn't defeat, or maybe it was, but at that time I was willing to accept that this was my life. Maybe all of the happiness, joy, achievements, and success was finally over for me. They say all things are seasonal.

December of 2018, I had a grandmother gain her wings and another being celebrated in her church during the same time. My daughter and I made a trip to Miami along with my parents to be a part of both the funeral and the celebration. While at my grandmother's funeral, I saw my biological father who I had not seen in well over 20 years. He didn't even recognize me when he saw me. I don't know if it was because of the depression, or the fact that so many years had passed. It felt like a dagger had went through my heart. As my eyes filled with tears, there was a huge lump in my throat. You know that feeling when you are full of pain and sadness but you do not know how to receive it or express it? That feeling that leaves you speechless. There was definitely an emptiness that I could not explain.

He was also seeing my 15 year old daughter at the time and he had no idea who she was. *Why did he not recognize her? Why did he not see me in her?* I don't know if you can even begin to imagine the feeling of not being recognized by your own blood, but I can only pray you never have to experience it. We hugged and exchanged well wishes, but it felt as if that chapter in my life had finally closed. There was no anger on my part. I am blessed to say later on, we reconnected and made the peace we never had. All was forgiven and a huge weight was lifted from my spirit. There were so many things that I held against him for so many years. None of that matters anymore. We now have a connection and a new relationship to build. God restores all.

A day or so later, we celebrated with my other grandmother. She was being honored in her church. Deep down, I was so happy for her; but my depression would not allow me to show that on the outside no matter how hard I tried. I know my Granny knew my heart. Once we arrived back home from Miami, my grandmother called me. The moment she said God told her to call me, tears began to fall from my eyes. I knew she had a Word for me. A Word that I needed. A Word that would give me some form of hope and maybe even a little joy. A Word that would allow me to pick myself up again and keep pressing forward. She began to tell me that God wanted me to know that everything was going to be alright

despite what I was feeling. She gave me 2 scriptures that He placed on her spirit to share with me. Psalms 91:1-16 and Numbers 23:19
Psalms reads,

> *"He that dwelleth in the secret place of the most High shall abide under the shadow of the Almighty. I will say of the Lord, He is my refuge and my fortress: my God; in Him I will trust. Surely He shall deliver thee from the snare of the fowler, and from the noisome pestilence. He shall cover thee with His feathers, and under His wings shalt thou trust: His truth shall be thy shield and buckler. Thou shalt not be afraid for the terror by the night; nor the arrow that flieth by day; Nor for the pestilence that walketh in darkness; nor for the destruction that wasteth at noonday. A thousand shall fall at thy side, and ten thousand at thy right hand; but it shall not come nigh thee. Only with thine eyes shalt thou behold and see the reward of the wicked. Because thou hast made the Lord, which is my refuge, even the most High, thy habitation; There shall no evil befall thee, neither shall any plague come nigh thy dwelling. For He shall give His angels charge over thee, to keep thee in all thy ways. They shall bear thee up in their hands, lest thou dash thy foot against a stone. Thou shalt tread upon the*

lion and adder; the young lion and the dragon shalt thou trample under feet. Because he hath set His love upon me, therefore will I deliver Him: I well set him on high, because he hath known my name. He shall call upon me, and I will answer him: I will be with him in trouble; I will deliver him, and honour him. With long life will I satisfy him, and shew him my salvation."

Numbers 23:19 reads,

"God is not a man that He should lie; neither the son of man that He should repent: hath He said, and shall He not do it? Or hath He spoken, and shall He not make it good?"

I highlighted these passages in my Bible and have read them every day since. It started to shine a little light over my situation but not fully cast out my darkness. People tend to think that one Word from God or one scripture immediately sets us free, but it is a process. First we must trust and believe. The miracle does not always come right away. We still have to do the work. Faith without works is dead.

It was at that moment when I finally went public on my social media and shared what I had been dealing with and how broken I really was. It was not for validation or anyone's approval. It was because someone out there needed that Word at that moment. God will send a Word through others. They needed to see that someone who had experienced what it was like to be on top could still be brought all the way down. That didn't mean anything was wrong. It's just life. Too often we're afraid and embarrassed to admit that life hasn't been easy for us. Let's be honest. We have all dealt with suffering and loss. We need to understand that even those who do well in life will still experience darkness. I believe that God uses us to show others His work.

After sharing my experience, I began to receive an outpour of messages thanking me for being transparent. I no longer felt inferior because of the cards life had dealt me. I felt like the façade had finally faded. Everyone on the outside looking in thought I had it all together. In reality, those same people had no idea what I was going through. I wasn't intentionally trying to hide the hardships I endured. I was learning how to deal with the lessons in life as they came. I was vulnerable and I was scared, but I knew my test could be someone else's testimony.

My days began to get better, but I still had a long road ahead of me. I would go an entire week feeling great. Then suddenly something would trigger my depression and I would instantly hit rock bottom. Depression is not something that is cured overnight. It is a long process. Admitting that you're battling it is only the first step. The key is not allowing yourself to feel defeated when you sink into that dark place. In those dark times, it's better to remember what it felt like when you were on the other side.

After a couple of months, I was over the pity parties. I knew I had to do something fresh and new. I had to get back to myself. Things were not perfect but I was excited again. I was slowly getting my passion back and gave myself room to make mistakes. Instead of looking to be free from depression in its entirety, I just made every single day count. I learned to live for today and not tomorrow, because we all know, tomorrow is not promised.

I started going back to church and tithing again. It felt good. I started to feel more at peace. I was finally getting out of the house and trying to keep myself busy. I was no longer thinking about what was behind me and began to focus on what was in front of me. My good days began to outweigh my bad days, but I was far from the end of my battle.

__Marriage__

Marriage is supposed to be a reflection of the relationship God has with the church. We must learn to do marriage God's way. Marriage was never supposed to be done with just 2 people. God was always supposed to be in the midst of it. God wants to give you everything you need for your marriage. Your relationship with God will dictate how all of your relationships will go. The real definition of marriage is dying to self for unity. The goal was always to become more like God. It's okay to ask yourself if you are pouring into your marriage from a dry place.

Ephesians 4:31-32 reads,

> *"Let all bitterness, and wrath, and anger, and clamour, and evil speaking, be put away from you, with all malice: And be ye kind one to another, tenderhearted, forgiving one another, even as God for Christ's sake hath forgiven you."*

Marriage is a journey of a lifetime. It isn't a sprint; it's a marathon. The faith of one person in the household can save the entire family. Are you praying over the Kingdom God has given you? God is a redeemer. Having a daily devotional life makes you better. You must stay prayerful every day. Always keep God in the center of your life. Satan's plan may have been to divide and conquer but God's plan is to unite and conquer. God's purpose in your marriage, family, and circumstances is to empower you. Heaven has a secret about your marriage. Heaven has a secret about your family. Heaven has a secret about your children. Heaven has a secret about your life. Sometimes your secrets are revealed and delivered in your darkness. As long as we stay in His presence, He can still reach us to restore us. God always wants to reveal the secrets to those whose hearts are open and willing to receive them.

Marriage is an institution of transformation. God wants us to become everything He created us to be and one of the things He uses to develop us is marriage. Marriage is one of His strategies to produce the best in us. It is the one relationship that challenges you to grow unlike any other relationship. It demands growth. You cannot have a strong marriage without a strong you. You cannot have a healthy marriage without a healthy you. You cannot have a whole marriage without a whole you. Nothing worthwhile is shaped by ease. Marriage will expose things about you that you would not see by yourself. It forces you to stretch, grow and become a better version of yourself. There is something about your spouse that will push out a better version of you. Not only does your spouse add to your life but they will bring something out of you too. When God blesses you with a spouse, you have in house accountability. The problem is many of us don't want to be accountable for our actions and choices in life.

Our job is to navigate through the tension in our marriages to create an incredible version of ourselves. Tension and confrontation in marriage can bring out the best in you if you allow it. Don't give up before you grow up or you may miss the best part. Marriage requires change. Life requires change. Parenting requires change. We cannot become as one without change. If you stay the course and navigate through the tension, then God will develop you and give you the ability to endure things that you couldn't do alone. That mountain in your life may seem bigger than you but I promise it won't be for long. God will do something on the inside of you to enlarge your capacity.

There is discipline that should allow the tension in your marriage to produce reflection and not projection. Read that again. We look through windows but a mirror forces us to look at ourselves. I had to learn to not become so caught up in searching for my spouse's flaws that I missed the opportunity to look at my own. Your maturity is connected to your spouse's imperfections. If they are perfect then there is no room for you to grow. The flaws and imperfections will pull out a Jesus sized version of you. Ask God who you need to become to navigate through the imperfections. If God gave you your spouse, then there is an anointing down on the inside of you to handle anything that comes your way. You have the power to break every chain.

Can I be honest for a moment? This is a very sensitive topic for me. Anything that has to do with my family touches my heart differently than daily life struggles. I will go to war for mine. The moment that war made its way in my home, all Hell broke loose. It was time to get my house in order.

I met my husband in 1995 when I was just 15 years old. I never knew he would be the one God chose for me and vice versa. We got married in November of 2000. We've since had 2 beautiful children. A young king and our growing princess. I must admit life always seemed to be perfect for our family. We had our share of everyday life struggles. I'm referring to things like sickness and death. The things you can't control. I would like to think we had it made but that was my ignorance talking.

There is a connection that happens in a marriage that produces a model of Christ in the church on earth. When the enemy feels He can get distance between the man and the woman, His goal is to delay what God is trying to do. Christian marriages should produce an image so amazing that it makes people want to get saved just from looking at it. Some of us have layers and tough skin that we bring into our marriages and families. It may be things that happened before our time that we have no control over. Ask the Holy Spirit how you can lovingly peel back those layers so that you can become one. God does not call us to change one another in marriage, but to become one.

If your marriage does not feel great in a season, it is okay because there is still purpose in it. Your job is to find out what God is trying to do through you. Love does not just die because love is eternal. Love is not just a feeling. It is committed actions repeated until your feelings catch up with your discipline. It is okay to disagree but it should never change your commitment to love. Love is what you do for one another despite what you feel. In marriage, you may feel as if you are not getting the love you deserve but what if your spouse is having a hard time loving themselves? You cannot give what you do not already have. If they are not loving you out of overflow, they may be empty on the inside.

God will unearth, unwrap and unveil some of the scabs but we must be patient to see our new identities emerge. Are you stepping into a new identity or are you to be patient while your spouse is stepping into theirs? Maybe you feel like you and your spouse are 2 different types of fruit but you must understand you are still in the same garden. If the enemy is attacking your family or marriage, it is because He knows that if you ever get on one accord, there is nothing Hell can do to stop what God wants to do.

My husband is the ying to my yang. He is my best friend. After all, we did grow up together. We did everything together. If I had to travel for work, he was right there with me and the same with him too. We often took family vacations and baecations. People would often tell us that they were inspired by us. They were inspired by the fact that we showed others real and true love does exist. We're an example that healthy marriages and two parent households where everyone got along together are real. We have always protected our kingdom. We learned to experience the hardships and triumphs together. We always cheer each other on and always remain in each other's corner. Whatever I wanted to do in life, he always supported; and I too supported him. Talk about being inseparable.

I believe that when God is ready to shift some things in your life, what once seemed perfect can be shaken up. When I first began to battle with depression, it was my husband that I felt the most sorry for. He was the one that had to be around me every day. Not only did he have to experience what I was going through, but also he had to deal with it. This was new for the both of us. No matter how hard he tried to make me feel better, it just did not seem like it was enough. Nothing seemed to satisfy the urge I had to get my joy back.

We took a trip in February of 2019 to the Dominican Republic. It was absolutely breathtaking. After about 3 months or so, life shifted again. I couldn't seem to catch a break. Depression struck again; but this time it was so much worse. I thought to myself, *"God why me?"* I barely made it out the last time. I had vowed to never to be in that place again.

Once again, I stopped leaving the house. I stopped being excited about my business. It felt like my life was on pause and I had no idea why. So I did what most would do. I got comfortable. I stopped showing up in my marriage and home. I was tired. I was exhausted. I was confused. I was over it. I even stopped going to church again. I wasn't angry with God. I was just lost and confused. I felt numb. I had no sense of direction. Everything I knew suddenly felt unfamiliar to me.

I can remember going to church one time and the pastor prophesying over my husband. I felt like God was sending a Word and I hung on to that for dear life. That Word gave me a little bit of hope, but that quickly faded. I began to accept my defeat and accept that maybe this was just my life. I contemplated suicide. As much as I know God, I was just as embarrassed to admit this is what I was dealing with. My flesh had its mind made up but my spirit knew that was not the way to go. I found myself thinking about how I was going to do it and where I would be. I just wanted it to be over. Quick and easy. *But who will find me? How would this affect them for the rest of their lives? How would they remember me?* These were the thoughts running through my mind.

In the midst of my thoughts of suicide is when things began to change in my marriage. My husband tried to force me to get help. However, I was ashamed. I was not supposed to be going through this. This was not how my life was supposed to be. I told him if he made me go, then it would be his fault if something were to happen to me. I put my burdens on him. I put him in the worst situation possible and I had to live with that. I hated myself for doing that to him. All I know is that I didn't want to be on this earth any longer. I felt as if I had already died on the inside but my flesh remained here on earth. Everything I once knew with my best friend suddenly felt like a memory. He was no longer happy, and neither was I. I wondered to myself, *"Where did we go wrong? What happened? Where did I drop the ball? How do we get back to what we had? How do we fix this?"*

At that moment, I was angry with God not knowing He had a plan the entire time. When I thought my marriage might be over, everything began to change. God has a way of orchestrating things in our lives so that we will either surrender to His will or be forced to fall at His feet. Maybe even be thrown at His feet. I think my situation was a little bit of all of the above. This was probably the worst time in my life. God shifted everything in my life. Things may have looked the same on the outside, but nothing was the same on the inside. I was at the lowest place in my life. My home didn't feel like home anymore. My husband looked the same but it was not him on the inside. That was not the man I married. *What happened God?* I wanted my life back! It was as if he had a shell around him and his heart became hardened. The pain was unbearable. I had officially experienced my very first heartbreak. This was worse than my father not being in my life. My husband was all I've known for 25 years.

We were just existing around one another. He didn't know what to say and neither did I. We had no words. We smiled around others but we were both broken on the inside. Nothing felt right in my life. I couldn't remember the last time we shared some of the moments I cherished. The times we would laugh uncontrollably. The times we'd stay up late and just talk. The times where the world around us would just disappear while we looked into each other's eyes. This was not like us. *Who were we becoming?* Awkward was an understatement.

This went on for several months. I felt like I was living in fear wondering if today would be the day we both agreed it was over. *Would today be the day I give up on my life, my family, and all I have ever known?* This was worse than the depression. It was depression on another level.

I started looking back at pictures we had taken a few months prior. It felt like they were taken in a different lifetime. I couldn't remember the last time I woke up without wondering if we would be together. I would have given anything to have it all back. I was willing to give my life. I began to wonder if maybe I had taken it all for granted. When you are happily in love, who takes time to question if the happiness and feelings would last? We had tons of friends that were once married and now divorced. Some even remarried again. *Was that going to be us? Has our journey come to an end?* Every morning seemed as if we were both putting on masks just to get through the day. We did not hate each other, but it seemed like we no longer knew one another. We were no longer the same people. *Was he changing or was it me? Could our children see that we were sad and unhappy? How would this affect their relationships as they got older?* My thoughts and emotions were constantly at war.

I think the hardest part was still trying to be positive in the world. Our children still needed us. I still had a team who counted on me. I felt like I was carrying the weight of the world on my shoulders. I was completely empty on the inside. Some were inspired by my positivity, some by my faith and even some by my marriage. Meanwhile, I was at war trying not to lose it all. I couldn't pinpoint the exact moment everything changed. It seemed to happen overnight. I know other couples who have gone through issues but I was not willing to accept mine. God didn't bring me this far just to leave me. I know some situations you cannot control and you must part ways, but I refused to go out without a fight. I was not a quitter. I wasn't going to allow the devil to take my life and I definitely was not going to let him take my family!

I knew I had a decision to make. I could either accept my defeat, let this tear my family apart, choose to remain unhappy and go on with life, or get on my knees and seek God for guidance. It's crazy how He speaks to us when we are still enough to listen.

My norm was no longer my norm. I was forced to dig deep inside and confront my battles, flaws, and insecurities. I had to become vulnerable. I studied the Word morning, noon, and night. I didn't watch TV or go out. I just wanted to draw myself closer to God. He began speaking to me in ways I could never have imagined. I started watching sermons on YouTube. I studied them. Crazy thing is, I was forcing those sermons to relate to my husband thinking the words being spoken were for him. I would tell myself, *"He needs to see this,"* in hopes that it would speak to his soul. I would ask God to give him the spirit of discernment. I failed to realize that if the Word was not for him, then it was not going to speak to him. This went on for several weeks. Nothing I was doing seemed to be working or getting better.

I was forced to dig deeper. I was praying, studying, and being obedient but I still didn't know what God was trying to tell me. *What was I missing? Am I not praying hard enough? Was my prayer too short? Why am I still crying myself to sleep every night? Why do I still feel empty? Why was I still having these dark thoughts? I knew the Word and how marriage is sacred in the eyes of the Lord, so why was He leaving me in despair in mine? Why weren't things better??* I prayed at night but when we woke in the morning it felt like God hadn't heard me. *Why didn't we both wake up happy today?*

I still had that selfish mindset of wanting everything to be perfect and whole again. I wanted it to happen my way and I wanted it now. I wanted my prayers to be answered for my own self gain instead of asking God what He was trying to teach me in this season. I was still angry. I knew what to do but it wasn't working. I needed to find out how He wanted to use me during this time. I wasn't going to receive what I had been asking for from God for until my assignment was complete.

Back to the drawing board I went. *Lord, what are you trying to get me to see?* Suddenly, the scriptures and sermons began to speak to my spirit. That is an indescribable feeling I can only pray that everyone gets to experience. It was a sense of peace like no other. When you ask God to speak to you, you'd better be ready for what He is going to reveal.

All this time my prayer was for God to use my husband and speak to him, but it was me He wanted to work on. I had to allow Him to have access to ALL of me including the areas I felt most vulnerable. The ones I hid from the world and from myself. The ones I kept in the dark.

Spiritually Out of Shape

Romans 12 reads,

> *"And be not conformed to this world, but be ye transformed by the renewing of your mind; that ye may prove what that is good, and acceptable, and perfect, will of God."*

God will snatch you back in line if you allow Him to. He will not force Himself on you. He is a gentleman. He just wants us to trust Him and surrender our will to His. It's a very hard thing. Trust me. I know all too well. No matter how hard we pray or how bad we want something, God will not allow it to happen if it is not a part of His will for our lives. I thought I was surrendering but I was still holding back parts of me. The parts I didn't want Him to touch, the parts I buried, but God is the creator of all. He knows us better than we know ourselves. We cannot hide from Him. He is made strong in our weakness. He works best with our mess. He does His best work in the dark.

As I began to dissect different sermons and messages, I realized that everything happens for a reason. Believe it or not, we are all exactly where we are supposed to be. Even our trials, heartaches, bondages and ground zeros. Our job is to dig deep down within ourselves. Nothing is worse than feeling like you are being punished when you thought you were doing a good job and being obedient. God does not want to take anything away from us unless it goes against who He has called us to be. He wants to multiply in our lives so that He can receive all the glory.

    We give the enemy too much credit, forgetting that God does not allow the enemy to do anything He has not approved of. I felt like my marriage was under attack and I no longer knew my husband, but God knew that if He shook something up that He could get my undivided attention. When He knows you will not move, He will force you to move by making you uncomfortable. The enemy is only good at playing tricks on our minds. He wanted me to think that things were over, but God put me in that position for a reason. Exodus 14 talks about how God hardened Pharaoh's heart so that Moses would perform a miracle and part the Red Sea to save the people. When I read this I thought to myself, *"If God is of love, then why would He harden anyone's heart?"* He always has a plan. In the beginning, I believed that it was the enemy attacking my husband but God orchestrated this chaos. If his heart was hardened towards me and the spirit of affliction was over my marriage, I would be forced to draw closer to God. Not only to birth His promise, but also to find the seed God had planted down inside of me. I was pregnant with purpose. Now I needed to figure out how it would all come together. I knew I had to get back into praying and spending time with God which revealed my flaws and insecurities. God allowed my life and home to feel as if it were being demolished. *What's in all of this for me? How is this working for my good?* I had these conversations with God to gain clarity on my next steps.

He began to reveal that in order for me to minister to His people, I had to go through it and endure the pain so that my testimony could be more relatable. I was angry. I was still confused and questioned God. *"Why are you allowing my marriage to struggle for this to happen? How does any of this make sense? How can I tell anyone God is real, and can still perform miracles, if He did not perform one for me?"*

Things didn't get easier. They actually got harder. I had to go through the test before I got the lesson. I couldn't speak on something I had not gone through. God was truly working in mysterious ways. Although I received the assignment, I still had to put my trust in Him for it to all come together. I was walking through this blind. I had to endure every step of the process while still feeling heart broken, confused and tired. I wanted to give up. I felt unworthy. Despite my constant internal conflict, I still had to surrender to Him. I was holding back because things weren't happening the way I wanted them to. It didn't make any sense to me. A part of me was still trying to have my own backup plan in case God's plan didn't work out. It felt like I was getting my tail handed to me. God had to back me in the corner.

Eventually, I gave in but I still had doubt in the back of my mind. It was only a little bit of doubt but it was definitely there. I began to align myself with God's purpose but things in my life still weren't fixed yet. The only thing I could think to do was pray harder and submerse myself in the Word even more.

Transformation is a process. It does not happen overnight. This is the very moment when people quit on their calling. They give up on who God called them to be. We begin to feel like our prayers are being unanswered but God wants us to stay the course and trust Him. If He revealed it now, it wouldn't make any sense because we wouldn't be able to handle it. He must first grant us the strength, tools, and strategies so when the time comes, we will see how He had His hand over us the entire time. Do not give up. Just be patient.

Every once in a while, He would test me. God wanted to see if I would go back to being complacent and stray away, or if I would have the discipline to manifest what He had given me. He wanted to see if He could trust me. I'll admit I failed almost every time. I was getting what I needed in the flesh but not in my spirit. Frustration was an understatement. I felt like I was taking 2 steps forward only to be knocked 50 steps back. Each time I let defeat set in, it allowed the enemy to come and manipulate my mind.

God continued to speak to my spirit that I was going to break generational curses, and that once I made it on the other side, I would be grateful for everything

I endured. I later heard a sermon that convicted my spirit. During this sermon, the pastor said, "God is working. Stop getting in the way and rushing Him." We tend to pray thinking that things aren't working because of what we see or do not see. I stumbled on the scripture about Peter while he was in prison in Acts 12. The people of the church were praying for Peter to be set free. They continued to worship and give praise even though they couldn't see what was happening on the other side. They had unshakeable faith. They had no idea God was already working on their behalf.

My prayer shifted. I started asking for God to show me on the outside what He saw on the inside. What was going on around me looked nothing like what He promised me, but God is not a man that He shall lie. I stayed in the Word day after day. I studied the Bible and yearned to be in His presence even though my house was out of order. My family felt like it was broken. Everything about my old life and what I once knew was gone. God only gave me enough to sustain me each day. That is where faith kicked in. He never allowed me to starve or go without but He filled my spirit just enough so that what once seemed uncontrollable began to seem bearable. It left me wanting for more. He was my shelter. He was my only peace in this situation. It was so hard not knowing what was to come. I tried to not focus on my circumstances and keep my eyes on the promise.

There was no peace in my house at the time so I struggled with understanding how I could birth something that would one day be a blessing to someone else. *How do you pour out from emptiness? How do you tell someone there is hope when your world seems to be hopeless?* Nothing was making any sense to me. I had fear of the unknown but I had to put all of my trust into Him. I continued to pray and ask God to keep my thoughts, mind, and heart aligned with His. I wanted to be in sync so that I didn't move unless He said move. I was tired of trying to do things my way. Nothing I was doing on my own was working. *This could not be life. God, you promised me more. You said I was the head and not the tail. You said that all things would work together for the good of those who loved the Lord. Note to self: "When you fall down, try again, but this time with God."*

I was against a giant I had never encountered, let alone defeated. I kept hearing God tell me I already had everything I needed. I continued to remind myself that God will use anything necessary to manifest the things He placed on the inside of me. I had to understand that God will place you in the wilderness so that He can mold you into the person He has called you to be. The wilderness is where you discover your gifts, potential, and purpose. The wilderness is also a place of pain, heartache, tears and suffering. Things need to be stripped away and old habits must die. There is no way to get around this. The most difficult part is trying to figure out how this would end, but our ways are not God's ways. Our thoughts are not His thoughts. A part of me wanted to go back to my miserable life. I felt like anything was better than this. *God where are you? Can you hear my prayers? Do you see what is happening to me?*

Rather than constantly making myself more miserable, I started to think about all the things I had gained while I walked in the wilderness. I had heard from God and discerned the voice of the Holy Spirit. He had given me the power and authority to speak life and death over things around me. He blessed me with strength I never imagined having and more creativity than ever before. Understanding the flaws and insecurities that were once holding me back, I believe I was slowly walking into a better me.

My daily routine quickly changed. I no longer had the urge to watch television or just scroll through social media like I used to do. I was burying myself in the Word. My appetite changed. Food alone no longer satisfied me. I just wanted to be closer to Him. I was finally giving God the time He deserved. I was giving Him my undivided attention. I started my day with prayer, worship, and devotion. I started each day asking God what work He had for me to do for His Kingdom. I wanted to know how I could serve those that were assigned to my life. I wanted to be a blessing for someone else. I realized my prayers were no longer about me and what I wanted. My prayers had transformed to how I could save someone else. I wanted to always be in alignment with the Lord because the moment we step out of the will of God, life becomes much harder without Him in it. We have to understand that God is intentional and He is never in a rush when it comes to working on you and working through you. He is so strategic it is almost mind blowing. I knew I had to be patient with what God was doing. Having patience is easier said than done. Each day I wondered if my life would go back to what was once normal. *Will everything be fixed?* I had to trust the process.

Remove from your mind the idea that you can be broken and still function. That's a toxic trait that could be passed down to your children and your children's children. We all have a responsibility to get back in shape. I don't mean physically, but spiritually. Get back into the Word. That is where you will find your purpose. God already has a plan to help you overcome your opposition. God says, "I can take everything that has happened to you and make it work for you." You're going to have to trust Him.

When your heart is tired, you have to hang onto what God said. Set some things in motion. Put businesses in the bloodline. Put success in the bloodline. Put authors in the bloodline. Put happy marriages in the bloodline. Put anointing in the bloodline. Put healing in the bloodline. Break depression from the bloodline. Put joy and happiness in the bloodline. God is going to give you wings for war.

I wanted to say I hated my life. The problem with admitting that would not only mean that I hated what God thought about my life, but also mean that I hated the plans He had for my life. Let me tell you, that is the trick of the enemy. We are a part of God's creation and all that He has created is beautiful and perfect in His eyes. We may stray away, some of us more often than others, but He loves all of us the same. His grace is sufficient. There is NOTHING you can do to make God change His mind about you. We are not that powerful.

When I have those moments I quickly remind myself that I am the child of a King.

- *I am wonderfully and fearfully made.*
- *No weapon formed against me shall prosper.*
- *I can do all things through Christ who gives me strength.*
- *I fear no evil. I walk with Christ. I am blessed and highly favored.*
- *My tongue is heavily anointed and the words I speak shall come to pass.*
- *I'm serving Hell notice.*
- *Darkness steps back when I walk into the room.*
- *I was given the authority to make Hell tremble and demons flee. I have the power to summon angels.*
- *Strongholds are coming down. Yokes are breaking. Chains are falling. Mountains are moving and the floodgates of Heaven are opening over my life and everything attached to me.*

I wrote these things in my prayer journal and spoke them over my life. I knew it was already handled. I was covered. God said no evil would conquer me and no plague would come near my home. I could be out running errands and would still speak these things under my breath. God hears all prayers. The enemy could no longer have me. Sometimes you have to remind yourself, especially when you don't feel like it. Remember your tongue is a powerful weapon. Say it over and over again. Don't believe me? I dare you to try it!!

    I wanted to see my spiritual DNA reproduce and amplify. I wanted a chain reaction. I had to ask God what spirit was reproducing and amplifying in my marriage and family. *What spirits are down on the inside of me that are at war with what God wanted to do in me? Lord, show me how to carry a Word and take care of the people you have assigned to me.* My marriage is a Word. My children are a Word. My family is a Word. He gave me a key to steward over. My anointing could not be fully effective until it had been tested to overcome opposition. Too often we want our next without the opposition.

    We have to be able to handle when God says no so we can receive when He says yes. When we distance ourselves from God, we lose the power of manifesting His promise. God doesn't anoint error or a path that hasn't been ordained. His steps have been ordered. God gave me the influence required to break open the door that He needed me to be the deliverer He called me to be. Life pushed and almost broke me until I finally surrendered to becoming the one who was desperate for God. What a mighty God we serve. He is so worthy to be praised.

Learn to stay under God's cloud so you can see properly. Confronting opposition can sometimes cause suffering before creating resurrection. You must first confront the issue. Then know how to surrender the issue. Let the best parts of you be resurrected. You can say things like "This opposition is not going to overcome me," "I'm speaking up over my opposition." Get specific with the enemy and declare that depression is going to let go of your mind. When it lets go, you're going to get your joy and peace back. Tell the enemy your marriage is going to flourish as a result of it. God shall supply all of your needs. You have cried your last tear over that situation. Get the tools to help wage war with the enemy.

If what you see doesn't look like what God said then don't give up. It doesn't mean it is over. You have to throw another seed at it and keep going. Throw another seed at your marriage. Throw another seed at your family. Throw another seed at that new business. Throw another seed at that book. Throw another seed at that degree. Throw another seed at that podcast. Throw another seed at that song. The promise is over your seed. The breakthrough is over your seed. Generational curses are going to break because of your seed. Every seed that fails will get you closer to the seed for your breakthrough.

If you have not seen what God promised, it's okay. Just know that you set something in motion. Set wholeness in motion. Set restoration in motion. Set resurrecting power in motion. Set revival in motion. Set your anointing in motion. Set healing in motion. Make a decision that whatever you set in motion, no one in your family will ever have to go through it again.

Some of you are lasting on your grandmother's prayers. When you set something in motion, now your children and your grandchildren can last on your prayers. Imagine what you can do when you start to see yourself the way God sees you. You can change your marriage. You can change your family. You can break those generational curses. Be mindful of what you allow to water you and what leaves you in drought. Stay in position because that is where God will protect you. That is where you will receive the promises and covering of God. Get back to your place in the wilderness that God has prepared for you. The wilderness is where you are fed, nourished and nurtured. It can be scary, but the wilderness is where you thrive. It's where you become creative and obedient.

Once you realize what you cannot do on your own, God will give you wings to accelerate your journey and obedience. There will be things that many had to work years towards but God will speed it up for you just to say He did it. Get back into position and stay there until He tells you to move. You will be given wings for your war in the middle of your despair.

When you feel like you have been thrown in the grave, remember that you still have resurrecting power. Your wings are on the way. Do not be afraid. We see that several times in the Bible. *"Be not afraid."* God will shrink your enemies and make ways for you that the enemy will not see coming. The enemy will not know they existed. The devil is counting on your ignorance. He's hoping that you will not discover your purpose and calling that God has over your life. That is the only reason He seems to be attacking and fighting so hard. God may not rescue you when you want Him to but remember He is still protecting you. Even when you do not see or feel Him. He will create a space that you may be harmed but you won't be broken. It's more important for you to gain strength. God is never a minute too early or a second too late. He is always right on time. It will always work together for your good.

There is always a seed buried in despair that has the key to our victory. I began to ask God what He would allow me to do in my marriage and family that would reveal His grace and glory into the world. I had to leave what seemed temporary to establish a new dimension. I had to change what was on the inside in order for it to become fully manifested on the outside. Miracles take place when you expose your weaknesses to God so that He can reveal His power. In life you may have to take the test first and learn the lesson later.

I didn't believe that my situation was desperate enough for the power of Jesus but I began to call on His name. *Jesus, help me to see my marriage the way you see it. Help me to see my family that way you see it. Help me to see myself the way you see me.* I needed His perspective in my lack. I had to stop focusing on the things I didn't have. I had to remember to whom I was connected. I had to remember who my Father was. I'm proof that the good, acceptable will of God still exists in marriages and families. Sometimes, we can't trust the way we're accustomed to thinking because our minds haven't been fully renewed.

When you think your marriage is over, ask God what He thinks. When you think there is no hope for your child, ask God what He thinks. When you think you have been defeated by depression, ask God what He thinks. Every attack has a time limit. Trouble doesn't last always. You may be in your wilderness right now, but remember, we must suffer with Him before we can reign with Him. You are a glory carrier. When you step into the room, darkness must move back because you serve a multiplying kind of God.

I knew I needed a miracle so that I could be someone else's miracle. I have an obligation to share what God has done in my life. At the end of the day, only the things we do for the Kingdom are going to last. I am a vessel. When people look at me I want them to see the grace of God. I want His glory to be exalted through how I live my life. My job is to become God's hands and feet here on the earth and bring His people back to the Kingdom. He wants to use those who are most passionate about what He has done in their lives.

The worst thing you can be to yourself is a coward. I took my story back from the devil and you can too. You must remember who wrote your story. One bad chapter doesn't mean your story is over. As long as you love what you have, you will have everything that you need. I had to get more radical in everything I did. I learned to create an environment for the blessings to take place in my life. The moment I made up my mind to make room for what God was trying to do in my life, I gained an understanding mindset.

God forced me into a deeper relationship with Him. The disappointment I was experiencing was to encourage my growth, not slow me down. He didn't answer my prayers when I wanted Him because the end goal was to seek Him, trust Him and elevate my mindset. I never lost my seed nor my purpose. He just changed the way I would receive it.

In this season, I thought I couldn't connect with God any more than I already had. I later learned I had to seek Him on a more intimate level. That required me to be stretched. If you haven't been stretched in a season in your life, then expect to be uncomfortable. He is the God that goes ahead of us and elevates the things we pray for. He is the God that has already made our crooked paths straight. He is the God that makes our broken lives whole again. It does not always look like what we may have imagined, but that doesn't mean it isn't going to blow our minds and rock our worlds.

Sometimes, God may give you a vision, but does not always tell you the fight that is attached to what He has for you. You have to learn how to love the resistance that comes along with your purpose. I knew I was too close to winning, so quitting was not an option. Right when you want to give up is when you are that much closer to your breakthrough. Keep going. You could lie there and die or you could get up and fight. I had to fight while crying. I had to fight while bleeding. I had to fight while suffering. I had to fight while confused. I had to fight while broken. I had to fight while empty. God was turning me into someone who knew how to get knocked down but also stay in the ring.

How many of you decided to give up when God did not show up the way you wanted? How many of you have given up because He did not come when you needed? When we have a need, it creates an opportunity for Jesus to expand His anointing and His power. My battle showcased His ability to reach more people. If God put you in it, tell yourself you refuse to lose. My marriage and family are a testament of God's grace and glory.

This is my winning season. It's okay for you to speak life into your situation. Your tongue and faith are powerful weapons. I challenge you to use them. Once God gives us our miracles, we can defend our right to have it. The enemy was attacking and dividing my family, but God was teaching me how to defend and protect what He gave me. I needed the Son of David to touch my home. When you get desperate enough to have Jesus touch your situation, you can break those generational curses. Your victory is guaranteed. You will win!

The longer we think we can control the outcomes in our lives, the more frustration we are going to experience in our journey of faith. God will not move just because we experience discomfort. Your faith cannot manipulate God's plan nor His timing. The love you have for God is proven in how we deal with His absence. Sometimes Jesus will leave us on READ. His love is not just about blessing us. His love is about us trusting Him even when we don't feel or see Him. He gets the glory when He steps in and turns our mess into a miracle. He makes the impossible possible. We think we need to see it to believe it, but God says we must believe it to see it. You can allow faith to propel you or fear to paralyze you.

His love is also proven by what He chooses not to do. Yup! You read that right. Your blessing could be in that no. He may not do what we want Him to do when we want Him to do it but that does not change who He is. It was my situation that gave the opportunity for a revelation. I had to see the disappointment before I could move into the next dimension. I had to look at my tombs of the dead things inside of me before I could understand and receive resurrecting power. Some things needed to stay dead while others needed to be brought back to life. It takes courage to admit that there is a tomb in your life. It takes courage to understand our flaws and imperfections. It takes courage to admit the things that are holding us back. It takes the same courage to admit we need help. I had to stop hiding behind my pride. On the inside, I was broken and defeated. I carried guilt and shame. I asked the questions: *"Why Me?" Why my marriage? Why my family? Why my life?* I had to open myself up and give God complete control.

It felt as if my life was falling apart and coming together at the same time. I was feeling fear and joy all at once. Fear is the space where God makes up the difference in our lives. I had to invite Him into my fearful and vulnerable places. If you want to learn how to have an undefeated mindset, consider these three tips:

1. *Expect miracles and make them your norm.*
2. *Don't worry about the surprises and unexpected attacks in your life.*
3. *Leave your tomb and don't look back.*

Psalms 37:34 reads, *Wait on the Lord and keep His way and He shall exalt thee to inherit the land: When the wicked are cut off, thou shalt see it.* Our job is to keep living out the pages in our lives. We need to ignore what the enemy tries to throw our way. It has been written. Stop worshipping at the altar of what was. There are no unexpected seasons to God. God was already setting the stage when I had no idea this time would even come. This situation was not about me. How

often do we make our attacks about us? It is about being a light for those who are counting on you. It is about the God who has trusted you to do something. I had to let go of who I used to be and step into who God called me to be. I never saw this fight coming. I was thrown in without a warning. I had no control over it but there is a process to the palace. A process to the promise. A process to the calling. What the enemy cannot destroy, He tries to distract. Stay focused.

Proverbs 3:5 reads, *"Trust in the Lord with all thine heart; and lean not unto thine own understanding."* Never allow your situation to determine your strength. What is crazy in one season will be counted as faith in another. We always think it's faith that we need to leave something, but sometimes, it's faith that we need to stay. Sometimes we are given the crown before we recognize the cost of getting it. There will always be a gap between your abilities and the promises of God. I had to start believing that God wanted to do something in me for the first time. We serve a God of expectations. I may be going through the same situation as my neighbor but I'm coming out differently. He may not have been able to do it for anyone else but decided to do it through me. The scene of my greatest storm was the setting for my greatest miracle. I had to go through the storm because it had to reposition me to where God needed me.

Nothing valuable in life is produced without pressure. How valuable is your marriage? How valuable is your family? How valuable is your career? How valuable is your purpose? How valuable is your calling? The fiery trials are painful but they're a part of the process to becoming a better you. There is no other relationship in life that forces you to look at yourself like marriage. When you feel the pressure, understand that God is trying to grow you. I needed to be a reflection of Christ in my marriage and my family. I was convicted and looking at the things that were happening in my life all wrong. God had to grow me up. There had to be an impartation, revelation and transformation. I embraced the growth I needed to become the person God created me to be. I embraced my healing.

The recipe for glory to glory is grit. When you have good seed in your family, the devil recognizes that and begins to attack. Will you go to war for your seed? I know I did. I was in a new season of being trained and groomed. Do you have the grit to receive what you've been praying for? When God chooses you, He equips you. Sometimes God places you in the wilderness so that others can watch you fight. When you defeat this wilderness you secure the Promised Land for everyone else.

I didn't realize I was a spiritual warrior on the inside. I was created to win and so were you. The wilderness revealed to me where my weaknesses and insecurities lied. It taught me how I could sabotage my own destiny if I lost focus. It made me desperate to pursue God. My relationship with Him is even stronger as a result of the wilderness. I felt lonely but I knew I was exactly where God wanted me to be. I had to learn how to like and worship in that dry place. When you are led by the Holy Spirit, there is an assurance that comes along with that.

I asked God how He wanted me to use the power of influence for those assigned to my life.. Marriage is a stewardship. Family is a stewardship. Money is a stewardship. Your job is stewardship. God has trusted us with those He loves. When God wants to do new things in your home, He will send the Holy Spirit to assess it. Everything will be inspected. Some things may even be demolished and renovated. He may even strip off the walls and tear down any and everything that does not look like Him. Your life will be in rehab and under construction. Do not leave the construction site too soon. Once He is done, you will be left with a mix of the old and new but He will leave you with just enough scars to keep you humble. Allow Him to rebuild the foundation in your homes. Otherwise, you will be taking a gamble if it is built on sand. It will be built with love, joy and peace.

God does some of His best work in the dark. He will often use your pain to produce your promise. The adversity you experience advances you. Prayer changes things. Sometimes God will allow you to be thrown into a prison. He does this not to punish you, but to bless you so that your blessing can be a blessing for someone else.

James 1:2-4 reads,

My brethren, count it all joy when ye fall into divers temptations; Knowing this, that the trying of your faith worketh patience. But let patience have her perfect work, that ye may be perfect and entire, wanting nothing.

God needed to develop me for where He was sending me. My dark place was where I found my purpose. Change your mindset. We are all the answer to someone's prayers. Before we can become a blessing to someone else, we have to ask God to deal with our selfish and grieving hearts. Ask Him to develop a generous heart in you. You must have a grateful heart so that you can give with the right heart. When God asks us to give to others, it is not to leave us out. He wants to ensure that if He gives it to you, He can get it through you.

    I was placed in a situation with pressure so I could remain still until He arrived. I refused to move in haste. Sometimes, if we leave where God has sent us, we may still see the fruits of our success; but He will take His hand from covering us. Trust me. I have tried to do any and everything on my own and nothing worked without God leading me. If there were another way, I would let you know but save yourself the trouble and get in agreement with God. How many times have you succeeded by doing something outside of the will of God and it lasted? I'll wait. Temporary success is not worth it. I want and need my fruits to last for generations to come.

God will do everything you can't do but will not do anything you can do. Faith without works is dead. He will hold you back until everything is ready before He allows you to walk through the doors He has for you. If you are not prepared, you will not have access. Get comfortable and ride the storm out. He will hide you on purpose while you are finding out who you really are. I was being hidden from the world while my entire life was under construction.

That prison you are running from or ashamed to be in is tied to your promise. The Lord knows how long to keep you there to protect what He has committed to your hands. Don't abort your promise because of your impatience. One of the biggest things I learned during this season was that I couldn't live in my feelings. I had to learn to celebrate even when I felt like I was losing. God had to trust me in one room before He could move me into my next room. The only difference was I walked into the room with more experiences, more lessons, and more wisdom.

Time after time, I felt unsure about my mission. I had to stay in His presence to get the reassurance I needed. I often questioned if it was Him who was really sending me there. He continued to give me the vision I needed to see, the focus to stay on course, the confidence to keep going, and the strategies to get where He called me to complete the mission. Everything that could be shaken, was shaken. There are times we ask God for more weight than we are ready to carry. It wasn't what I went through, but why I went through it. What the enemy meant to be a trap was actually my path. Everything that made me afraid was not the devil. Some of the things that were sent against me was not to destroy me. Everything I went through was to deliver me. I came through saturated and overflowing with the glory of the Lord.

When God tells us what He requires of us, we often tend to interview our blessing. I know I do. I had to search for the discipline to grow into my blessing. I was put in this position to depend on Him. We have to stop looking at our sufferings as punishment. Everything we endure is because God allows it. If we draw near to Him we will find out why. He cannot give us all He has in store for us at once because we have to learn to enjoy the journey of not being in control. You cannot be God of your life. Know your position and who is in control.

I had to give up everything that was normal to produce what God placed on the inside of me. I could no longer keep pretending I did not hear what He spoke to me. Has God revealed something to you that you keep ignoring? Something that you think is totally out of your comfort zone? Something that you feel you are nowhere near qualified for? Does it tug at your spirit? Do you keep thinking about it even when you are trying not to think about it? He is going to keep knocking until you answer. He won't force it, but He will always let you know it is available to you. He will never change His mind about you. You just have to be ready to receive it.

If you can endure the wait then you can endure the promise. The only way to get to the end is to know that God will see you through. Open doors can appear closed, but all we need to do is turn the knob. He taught me by the experiences and obstacles He placed in front of me. I needed to understand what this brokenness and lack was trying to teach me. Sometimes we have more faith in our insecurities than we have in the God who created us. I had a weapon that I didn't know existed, let alone how to handle it. I did not feel qualified but I was set on following the voice of the Lord. God told me He had given me the picture that He had in mind for my life according to His purpose and His will. Many times we sabotage ourselves because we only build by what we see. It is hard to believe God is in it when it doesn't feel good. But remember, we have been given the authority to overcome every wicked thing that rises to oppose us.

My obedience is what allowed me to become successful. The work that He was doing through my life began to drown my insecurities. I learned to risk being uncomfortable so that I could become unstoppable. There comes a time in our lives when we need to stop and ask God who He is calling us to be. Look around you. The time may be now. *What does your life look like? Is God trying to tell you something?* I had to prepare myself to have the type of character to maintain who God was calling me to be. He was going to use my brokenness to reach back and touch a soul that looked much like mine.

When our purpose is unfulfilled, we leave the next generation with some Goliaths that we were supposed to slay. The Lord will agitate our hearts until we step into the fullness of what He puts inside of us. Jesus cannot do many miracles where there is a lack of faith. Faith is the road we must take to get from a life that is purposeless to seeing a life full of purpose. Faith takes us from the wilderness to the Promised Land. The land of more than enough. I felt as if I was going through a season of significant loss and transformation. I knew my blessing was on the way. Purpose is not only about God using your skill but it's also about God using your story.

God wanted me to have my own experience with Him that I could not have without being tested. He was training me to build me up. You have no idea what God can do through a single seed planted in faith. If He met all of our expectations, He would never have the chance to exceed them. My marriage will be a testament of God's grace and glory that healthy marriages can last today. I needed to be retrained by God to hear His voice and follow His guidance. Sometimes our promises are not just given to us. Sometimes you have to fight for them.

God can restore what has been broken and use for others to be blessed. That is what you call grace. Grace is unmerited and undeserved. I realized I couldn't control what was happening in my life. I had no control over this season trying to do things my way. My desires required a bigger supply of Jesus that I had not quite reached. The odds seemed against me, but Jesus was still on my side. I thought things would be easy when I heard from God. My situation looked hopeless but I had to hang on even if it meant I had to do it from chains and bondage. *Jesus be a fence*. I refused to allow these chains to hold me down and lock me in this prison. I had to face everything that was coming my way with confidence while reminding myself that even in the darkest moments, God was with me. Everything would work out for my good.

It was not about the end result but more about the process. I knew I was going to come out of this thing bruised, wounded and scarred. My obedience and perseverance would eventually provide fruit. God wants those around us to become elevated because of who we are and what He has done for us. Speak the things that are not as if they are currently happening. Do not allow the challenges of your faith to keep you from having access to God. I had a faith that Hell could not ignore. My faith was going to be recognized. If we do not exercise our faith, we will live below where God has called us to live. It starts with acceptance. Only then will you have access to the Holy Spirit. We must take action to use our authority to fulfill what God has called us to do. Your repeated acts of faith establish your God-given authority on earth so that you may live in abundance.

Luke 10:19-20 reads,

> *"Behold, I give unto you power to tread on serpents and scorpions, and over all the power of the enemy: and nothing shall by any means hurt you. Notwithstanding in this rejoice not, that the spirits are subject unto you; but rather rejoice, because your names are written in Heaven."*

When God wants to heal your fading faith, He gives you something tangible to focus. He specializes in taking the things that others discount in broken and messy situations, and turning it around for your good.

Philippians 4:6-9 reads,

> *"Be careful for nothing; but in everything by prayer and supplication with thanksgiving let your requests be made known unto God. And the peace of God, which passeth all understanding, shall keep your hearts and minds through Christ Jesus. Finally, brethren, whatsoever things are true, whatsoever things are honest, whatsoever things are just, whatsoever things are pure, whatsoever things are lovely, whatsoever things are of good report, if there be any virtue, and if there be any praise, think on these things. Those things, which ye have both learned, and*

received, and heard, and seen in me, do: and the God of peace shall be with you."

When God gave me my Word, I began to worry and take this walk which made no sense to me. Carrying weight that didn't belong to me. Being stretched was not easy. The growth that was required felt unbearable. At this point, you can only be still with the Word He has given you. Being pregnant with a purpose but waiting for it to come to pass. Do you stand on the Word of God or the reality of your situation? The setback I thought I was experiencing was actually a setup for all He had for me. God loves making a way when it seems as if there is no way. As believers, we can't be bothered when it seems like doors are shutting around us. That is God's specialty. He does not like to be figured out. Trust me. I tried! He does not operate on our schedules.

What was going on in my marriage and family was going to turn my mess into a message. God was taking what was happening to me and allowing it to touch the world. This will allow others to become saved, healed, delivered, and have freedom in His Kingdom too. He saw all of my flaws and faults, yet He still chose me. He was the strength in my time of weakness. I continued to worship in my storm. I was right where He wanted me to be. Just when we want to give up in life, God will always come through and make a way.

We are blessed so that God can be worshipped. It changes the trajectory of people's faith to know that God is real. Sometimes it is to bless those who are far from Him. Too many people in this generation have lost their religion. You don't need to be whole to know God and experience His grace. Remember grace is undeserved. He works better in the middle of our brokenness. The things you are blessed with can be the very thing which will allow God to reach someone else. John 3:16-17 reads,

> *"For God so loved the world that He gave His only begotten Son, that whosoever believeth in Him should not perish, but have everlasting life. For God sent not His Son into the world to condemn the world; but that the world through Him might be saved."*

God uses us so that the world will know Jesus. I had to trust God when I couldn't trust myself. I was still serving Him even when nothing around me looked like what He promised me. Our worship, prayer, and praise is most powerful when He disappoints us. When we disappoint the Lord, grace is still given to us. Even through all of my mistakes and shortcomings, my relationship with God required some reconciliation. I was not always deserving but His grace is sufficient. God refuses to live in our expectations, especially when they are lower than what He has for us. When He gives us what we ask, He wants us to worship the One who gave it to us and not the thing that He gave us. When we keep our hearts in the right place, He can trust us with another level of glory. Even our buried prayers still reach Heaven's ears. His power has access to dead prayers. I needed the spirit of God to hover over every prayer that came from my mouth.

I had to learn how to straddle the fence of earthly living and Heavenly thinking. On earth, we may be a mess, but in Heaven we are already healed. I was taking all of my beliefs and throwing it in the direction of what God said to me. *I want to be a vessel for what God is doing on the earth.* Sometimes God forces us to grow through affliction. Every promise has a set of problems attached to it, just as every problem has a promise attached to it. In my situation, my problem came before I saw the promise. Pain comes along when God is taking you to the next level. I needed that place of bondage so that I could be everything He called me to be.

Affliction was my teacher. It forced me to multiply and grow. I had to look at my season with fresh eyes and ask God what He was trying to multiply on the inside of me. He will build your life through affliction. In a moment, His grace will come rushing in like a flood. The only thing it takes to walk into the freedom and abundance that has been promised in life is putting our faith in Jesus Christ. God has an inexhaustible capacity to forgive and bless.

It's hard to be patient while He's executing His plan. The secrets of the land are with those who fear Him. When you have a hunger for God that keeps increasing, He continues to reveal secrets about you and your life that are already settled in Heaven. When He speaks a Word in the natural, it is already completed in Heaven. We need a partnership with God to manifest what He has said and called us to do here on earth. The only thing that can hinder His Word from being manifested is when we allow ourselves to come in agreement with the enemy. Walk in your authority and know that the Lord is near.

God placed something on the inside of me that the world needed and it was time for me to pour it out. You walk in boldness and confidence when you carry the Word of God. As long as you stay in alignment, you will be victorious. He will always defend you and snatch you out of danger. If He doesn't snatch you out, then He will prepare you for the battle with the right tools and strategies needed to conquer and overcome.

God is always looking to see which vessel on earth would believe and trust Him once He reveals who they are in His eyes. Remember, He has already finished whatever He calls us to start. He speaks from a place that is already established. We just need to walk it out. What is established in Heaven does not always mirror what is on the earth. Our prayer is to ask God what He has established in Heaven. Ask God what He said about you and He will begin to reveal what is already done.

He sent every single one of us to solve a problem. There is a calling on our lives that is a solution to the chaos around us. Whatever God has called us to do matters. We are necessary. If you do not see what you do as valuable, you will mistreat and abuse your calling. There is no loss in God.

When God calls you it may feel like an interruption. It always seems to happen at the wrong time in our lives. It will strip the limitations on how you perceive yourself. You will have to unlearn what you have always known. You will feel as if you are in unfamiliar territory, but God always says "Do not be afraid!" We cannot judge the whole book in our lives when we are only midway through it. There will always be a connection to what you think you have lost and what God is calling you to. He will begin to unfold the layers of what He is doing when we seek His presence. I asked God to start showing me my life through His eyes. When God sends you to a place, He sends you to pour out something until there is an overflow. There are empty vessels in the world that we need to fill. I would be lying to you if I made it seem like any of this was easy. It was never meant to be easy, but it is necessary.

I began to think to myself, *"How can I create something great when I did not see greatness around me?"* I had to stop with the pity parties because no one was attending them. It was only me and the enemy. God had never let me down before. *What would make this any different from my last battle, my last struggle, my last trial, my last storm, my last desert, my last restless night, my last set of tears I cried?* The only way to get stronger is to allow Him into our weaknesses. Sometimes you have to go to war even when you're feeling weary. I was determined to see God even while facing an unexpected attack. God was my only way out of this. I had to pray about a strategy, pray for the wisdom, and pray for guidance to see me through. I didn't choose this battle; it chose me. The nature of our battles determine the nature of our strategies.

If it is God who gave it, then it is on us to protect it. One of my many jobs is to steward over a marriage and family God placed in my possession. My marriage belonged to Him. My family belonged to Him. They were just assigned to my life. I didn't know how to fix any of this but my eyes stayed on the Lord. I had to change my focus to win this fight. I had to stop being fixated on how big the problem seemed and praise God on how great He was.

Too many times we fight battles that are not ours to fight. We go to war unprepared and unequipped because we failed to seek God first. It was never about the power of my own strength. It was about the power God had already placed on the inside of me. Sometimes, it takes more faith not to fight back and allow God to be great in our situations. It was so hard for me to stop trying to manipulate God's plan. Sometimes we just need to let God lead the way. We need to learn to fight with focus and intention. We fight against what we see, but the fight isn't against flesh and blood. It is a spiritual warfare. If it's too big, it doesn't belong to you. Give it back to God! I was constantly stressing and worrying about something that was never meant for me to defeat alone. Instead, I just worshipped and allowed God to be God. He wanted His battle back. *Greater is He that is in me than He that is in the world*. I had to get in position and stay there to be delivered by the Lord.

You may have to face it, but you will never have to fight it alone. You may get bitten but you will not be beaten. Every time the enemy thought He had me, I shook it off and kept pressing. I have the scars to prove it. If it had not been for God, I would have never made it through. God didn't shake up my prison for me to get out. He shook up my prison for me to get in. Whenever you start praising God, He will come into any situation. Hell has never made a prison that God could not break into.

There were times I felt as if I was paralyzed. Everything around me seemed to be moving but I was not going anywhere. Although I did not think I was moving, God was. We must have a heart for God. He wants to know if He can trust us to carry out His assignment. *Can we be trusted to carry the weight of His glory? Can we be trusted with what He has established and ordained here on the earth?* I was already pregnant with my purpose by the time I got my calling. We are appointed by God to be a part of His agenda. God loves us all but He doesn't trust everyone equally. Trust must be developed and earned. Our hearts must be fully committed to Him. When building the Kingdom of God, you are actually building yourself and revealing the fruit of the Holy Spirit. We establish our obedience to God by first establishing the Kingdom of God here on earth.

The enemy only has access to us if we remain unfocused. The most authentic version of who we are is in the Word of God. He is always seeking those who can handle the weight of being revealed. *Can He trust you to show you who you really are?* Our hearts are our greatest weapons. It is okay to be a little afraid of what God is calling you to do. Just don't allow fear to cripple you. The process of faithfulness shows you the impact of the hand of God. Impossible situations is where our faith is born. I realized I couldn't help God get me to where He wanted me to be. I had to not only trust the process, but also value the experiences and lessons I was learning along the way. We must learn to wait on God.

God speaks to all of us about His visions but when we only focus on what we can see, we get out of alignment with what He has said. Nowadays people are posting and doing things for performance rather than purpose. In the area that we are waiting to receive God's goodness, is the same area where our beliefs and disbeliefs have to change. If we want what we are receiving to change, we have to stop accepting what we do not want. You may feel lonely in your walk with God but understand you are right where you are supposed to be. We serve a jealous

God. He adores that one on one time with each and every one of us. He often tends to separate us from the world to develop us.

When you are aggressive without a Word from God, it doesn't matter how you layout your plan. It doesn't matter how well thought out your blueprint and strategy may appear. If it does not have His backing, timing or direction, then it will not last. When you are stepping out of who you used to be into who you are becoming, things have to change. There will be a shift. Your environment has to shift and change. Your habits have to change. Certain things and people will have to be removed. The things that were once in a certain place, God has to remove in order for you to have a fresh perspective on who you are becoming. Old things have to be removed to make room for the new. Your capacity will have to be stretched. Even your mind will be stretched. There will be a void but that is when God will step in and fill that void with a divine exchange. The hardest part is not knowing when it will be filled. God is in control. He will work it out.

It is always hard to sit still during transition while you are threatened by opposition from the outside. Transition is the most significant place of opportunity and the most vulnerable place for insecurities. God is very active on the journey during your transition, if you are paying attention. Some of the greatest things that He will reveal in your life will not be on your vision board. Jesus doesn't always meet our expectations because He wants to exceed them. Many times we will receive a blessing that we didn't think to request. You can't take hold of what is new while you have a death grip on what is old. It's not what happened that triggers our anxiety, it's how we think about it. Doing so allows the enemy to get into our minds.

When we give weight to the promises of God and realize He is always in control, the things we were once worried about suddenly become irrelevant. Do not allow your situation to contaminate your spirit. When the enemy comes after your destiny, His first step is to set up a stronghold in your imagination. You will have to hold on to the promises of God through the storms of life. After you survive the storm, you have to find out why you survived. *Can you praise God for the result of a situation that is not yet resolved?* I had no choice but to survive during this season so that God could prove His power. I didn't have to like the event to celebrate the result. Perseverance is the only thing that would allow my faith to grow and enable the opportunity that was ahead of me. You're not a hostage in your situation. You are a weapon.

While the wind was controlling my boat, God was controlling the wind. If He allowed it, we can accept it. I'm not saying you have to like it but stay the course. The same place we are injured is the same place our purpose comes forth. It had to happen the way it did. Even the mistakes. Even the tears. Even the suffering. God needed me here right now. The storm stripped away everything I didn't need so that I could know the essential nature of who He made me to be. I was no longer going to carry dead weight into my new season. Maybe a door closed in your life that upset you, but God closes doors so that we will not spend years of our lives in the wrong rooms. He is so amazing and worthy to be praised! Thank Him for your open doors and don't forget the ones He went ahead of you and closed.

Philippians 1:20 reads,

> *"According to my earnest expectation and my hope, that in nothing I shall be ashamed, but that with all boldness, as always, so now also Christ shall be magnified in my body, whether it be by life, or by death."*

We can't fully experience the purpose of God with our minds on the past. You may feel like you went to sleep in a prison, but you are going to wake up in a palace. The process of finding out who we are becoming takes us through the prison. God wants to make sure that He can still touch us even while we are still in the prison. *Does God still have access to you while you are in your dry place? Can you tap into your purpose while sitting in your prison?* What may look like a prison to some, is a palace for others. It is all about your perspective. *Are you viewing your season as bad or do you know that something much better is on the way?*

People can be drawn to you because they sense the presence of God around you. Your influence is intimidating to the enemy. He doesn't go after the sheep. He goes after the shepherd. God may take you through a situation because He can use it to reach others in that very same situation. The enemy is always trying to get you as far away from your calling as possible. The devil already knows who you are and who you belong to. He knows the power you possess. He just hopes you never discover it.

There may be times that God will allow the enemy to shake you to get rid of your pride and rely on Him. That is one of the very things I had to deal with. Too prideful to let God handle it. Too prideful to give Him full control. Too prideful to admit I couldn't figure it all out by myself. I had to get to a point of stillness for God to reveal me. I had to endure the pride, the disappointment, the anger, the grief, the bitterness, the heartache, the pain, the tears, the suffering, the guilt, and the depression. He is not looking for who we pretend to be. He is looking for what we really feel. Until that comes to surface with acknowledgment and submission, God can't help us. Transformation is the renewing of the mind. Until we are aware of our insecurities and flaws, the demolition and rehab process can't begin. We must be stripped of the things that are displeasing to God, or the things that don't look like Him, before we can get to the point of being all He has called us to be. He can't do anything with the fake version of us. I was operating from a place of fear and had to become aware of that. The enemy came in and attacked when I was at the weakest point in my life. My vulnerability led Him right into my home, in my mind, in my family and in my marriage. The devil touched everything and everyone around me. Everything I was supposed to steward over. Everything that meant the world to me.

The Backside of Better

I believed my life was only sustained by good works. God isn't interested in what we are doing if it doesn't reflect our relationship with Him. I began to pray and ask God to search my heart and make me more like Him. I asked Him to uproot anything that didn't look like Him. He knew He could use this very situation to bring me to a place of humility so that He and I could walk together again. He wanted to be the priority in my life. I neglected to do the things I once did. I was doing what I believed was right at the time but God wanted more. He wanted to mature me in His love. He allowed what seemed like chaos in my life to get me where He needed me to be. He was using pain and suffering to mold me into the person He needed me to become.

My walks with Him allowed me to mature into the person who could understand His ways. I'm still learning today. He can never be figured out. This didn't happen overnight. This didn't happen until I surrendered and stayed in His presence. There are things about myself that I wasn't aware of that were revealed to me. He revealed things I never knew were hindering me. God was never after my marriage or my family. He was after my heart. He knew where to allow the enemy to attack to get my attention. I had to repent and submit to His will. I had self-righteous behavior. It needed to be broken from my spirit before He could use me.

He needed me to see the person I saw when I looked into the mirror. He needed me to meet the person He always knew was within me. The version of me I couldn't see. The daughter of a King. The daughter who was fearfully and wonderfully made. The daughter who was perfect in her Father's eyes. The daughter who was anointed. The daughter who was protected. The daughter who could do anything. The daughter who was not afraid of evil. The daughter who could move mountains. The daughter who would break generational curses. The daughter who could summon angels. The daughter who had a hedge of protection around her. The daughter who could speak life into her situations. The daughter who was healed by His stripes. The daughter who was covered in His blood. The daughter who wore His spiritual armor. The daughter who was filled with the Holy Spirit.

When God is preparing something new for us, there has to be a breaking point. Dead things have to fall off before we can walk into our new identities. God is invested in who we become. Nothing made sense to me when this attack occurred, but day after day, the more I stayed in His presence, the more He revealed. It was like following the breadcrumbs. It almost felt like I was on a scavenger hunt towards my destiny. In the beginning, I wondered where God was. I thought He had forgotten about me. I thought I was being punished. I thought this was just my life. I thought my better days were behind me. I later realized, God will give the command of what is needed to later birth what is to become. I was in the process of being pruned, developed, and prepared. God isn't looking at what He has given us to steward over. He is looking at who we must become for what we have been given. He had to humble me but He was with me in the storm the entire time. I wasn't in the wilderness alone. I wasn't in the prison by myself. I just had to stay near Him to hear His voice and allow the Word to be the light of my path. At this time I realized God was actually my storm. It was what I needed for my identity in Him to come forth.

There is a strength that comes when you know that even in your prison, you are still in the hands of God. Even though it seemed to be out of my control, it was never out of His sight. He used this entire situation to tell His people that whatever we are going through in life that seems to be chaotic and unstable is no match for Him. He is STILL in it. God had a plan all along. He uses things to build our lives that are often outside of what we think He should use. Believe it or not, I honestly thought I was exempt from suffering. I thought as long as I always did good or had a good heart, this type of turmoil would never come my way or hit me this hard. I had a lot of growing up to do. God checked me real quick. It is those that suffer with Him that are actually closest to Him. There is so much more to life I was missing out on until I decided to walk closer with God. We think we have our lives all figured out and that things that happen to us are just by coincidence, but until we have a more intimate relationship with Christ, we are suffering in our own ignorance. There is something about pain that begins to reveal the layers of who we really are. In order for God to walk with us, He needs to get to our core.

      He never wanted anything from me except my heart. Once God had that, the both of us could shake up this world. My spirit was mourning a version of me that was standing in the way of who He was calling me to be. Serving God isn't what we do only when life is great or we're feeling our best. We must recognize that we can still serve God in our pain and our loss. That is when restoration begins. In order for us to walk it out, we must become someone first. Everything that comes our way, God is in it. If it gets to us, He allowed it. I had to stop looking at my situation like I was the victim and ask God what He was trying to teach me. *God what do you need me to mourn in my flesh?* I needed to see, but at that point, I knew I could no longer rely on myself. My ways were not His ways. The molding and transformation was a process. It was long and enduring. It was frustrating but faith kept me going to remain obedient.

      Worthiness had nothing to do with what I could do for God, but what He could do for me and through me. He taught me how to allow the Holy Spirit to be my strength. During the moments when I felt least capable of doing anything is when I finally heard from the Holy Spirit. The answers I was praying for didn't come when I wanted it nor when I felt like I was ready. It didn't come until God said I was ready. I had to go through the process and understand its full entirety before it would all make sense.

When we are seeking God, let it only be because our hearts are after Him, and not because of what we can get from Him. That is where I often fell short but His grace is sufficient. There are some things that God will purposely not respond to. God is not a formula. There's no way we have Him all figured out. We can pray for our desires as long as we are seeking from our hearts with no selfish gain. He can see a pure heart that He can speak and respond to. It wasn't until I could come to Him with no selfish intentions that He answered me. What He has for us already belongs to us, but we must first look like the person who can steward it properly.

I will never understand how God moves but I know I don't want to do anything unless He is moving with me. After walking closely with Him, He began to reveal more secrets. I had to mature in my relationship with Him before He revealed why everything was happening and why He allowed it. There were some things I didn't have the capacity to receive. Had He answered my prayers sooner, it may have destroyed me. I wouldn't have been equipped with the lessons and experiences to share such a powerful and meaningful testimony.

He is so intentional and strategic. I later realized that I was never ready for what I thought I was asking for. He gave me peace and grace to keep me moving forward. Day after day, week after week, He only gave me enough to sustain me. Just enough to keep going but keep me coming back for more. I had to trust and surrender. I had to be honest with God and acknowledge that I couldn't do this on my own. I needed to let go and let God call the shots. I had to take my hands off of it and open my mind. I needed to see things from a new perspective. This drew me even closer to Him. I was eager to learn more. I was eager to hear Him speak. I was eager to see His grace. It was already working for my good and I had no idea.

Healing starts when we can say, *"God this is where my reality is but what is your perspective?"* The answer to my prayers was my own deliverance. It was through self-awareness. I was focused on the "what" and not the "why." My reason why was so much deeper. I couldn't win this battle until I knew the battle I was fighting.

I didn't want to start this book until I knew how the story would end. I thought to myself, *"If I didn't have any closure, where would it leave the thing God had called me to produce?"* The only instructions He gave me was to be obedient. The rest would unfold for the story to come together. It wasn't my husband. It wasn't my marriage. It wasn't my family. God never wanted to tear my family apart. It was me all along. It was my testimony. It was my story He wanted. I needed to be delivered. He never ceases to amaze me. The very thing that I was afraid of losing was the method that allowed God to manipulate and later reveal the answers to my prayers and my purpose. Something I would have never discovered otherwise. I told you the prison would turn into a palace.

God couldn't do anything for me if He and I weren't in agreement. This is why it is so important to stay under the hand of God and not live life for our own will. I feel so much more peace in my life when I encounter Him no matter what giants I may be facing. His power is released in agreement. The storm only came to reveal the storm that was on the inside of me all along. Jesus has won yet again!! Had my prayers been answered right away, I would still have conflict in my heart. Conflict that I denied. Conflict that I never knew existed. Conflict that would have hindered me in my life. Conflict that would keep me from the promises of God. My heart wouldn't have been pure. I wouldn't have been the person God knew I was supposed to be. I would have never met the version me that He created. My storm was ordained. The storm was never meant to be the problem I perceived it to be. The storm and war in my heart was the real issue. God orchestrated everything. He knew exactly when, where, and how it would all take place. He knew how much I could handle although it seemed unbearable to me. I needed to be healed so that I could live an abundant life. The storm was used to convict me so that He could mold and transform me. I was in denial.

    I was talking about God without actually talking to God. This relationship allowed me to see and experience a side of God I had never known existed. In my 40 years of life, I thought I had Christ all figured out. I wasn't even scratching the surface. I had to submit myself, my family, and my marriage before God with a humble heart so that He could reveal who He needed me to be in their lives. I had to be honest with myself. I couldn't share my story without the experience. It had to come from my heart. It had to come from my broken place. It had to come from suffering. It had to come from my wilderness. It had to come from that place of pain. You can't tell a story that you have not endured on your own. I couldn't share my testimony without being tested. I couldn't share something I had never gone through. It wouldn't be an authentic experience. Everything about it would be false. I couldn't share my flaws and issues had I been unaware of their existence. I had to stop being a fan of God and learn to be a disciple.

    Through every up and down, I became more rooted in the truth. There is nothing we can do that will convince God to change His mind about us or what He has called us to do. I had to meditate on His law and the Word day and night. Understand, I had to be built up for this. I had to conquer and overcome the war that was within myself. The battles I fought with daily. I could have never done this on my own. I was not going to see God's plan until I walked through everything needed to get me where I am today. God was everything I needed Him to be to get me to where I was supposed to be. He could have easily answered my prayers and established me in my truth but God also desires to spend time with us and build a relationship. Look at all the things I would have missed along the way. Each time I received a Word, I got to sit with God and spend more time with Him. The only peace I felt was in His presence.

I finally got to a point in my journey where I could hear from the Lord and understand when the Spirit spoke to me. If I didn't receive anything else during this season, that was a miracle in itself. I became stronger than I would have ever imagined. I was able to rid my body of the things that were toxic to my life, flaws, and insecurities. Those weeds needed to be uprooted before something beautiful could blossom. I had to endure the storm and sit in my wilderness for my story to unfold.

A cake wouldn't be a cake without all the ingredients. A cake can't bake properly without the right temperature and timing. My cake wasn't ready when I wanted it to be ready. It wasn't time for my celebration when I thought I was ready to celebrate. Things had to be sifted. Things had to be stirred up. Things had to be mixed. Things had to be poured. Ingredients had to be added. I needed just the right amount of oil to be measured out. Only God knew how hot to make the oven and how long to leave me in there. He knew how much heat I could take and how long I could endure it. I couldn't come out too soon or the cake wouldn't be absolutely perfect in His eyes. I had to experience the entire process.

    God gets all the glory. Every time I thought I knew the ending, God was actually still working. The journey continued. His plans were never my own but He knew it would all work together for my good once I made it on the other side. This changed me. My old life had to die including my old ways and bad habits. Passion is produced through your Hell. While other families may have fallen apart, God used mine for His glory. Every storm eventually runs out of rain. You're not staying in your current situation. Do not fear the change that is necessary in your life. Change is hard but change is required.

This book was written in a real life timeline. I actually thought my family and my marriage was falling apart when God told me to write this book. If I'm being honest, I was terrified of the ending. He was never trying to tear my family apart, but it was necessary for the manifestation of my assignment and what you are reading today. This piece was written by the Holy Spirit. God allowed me to be His mouthpiece, His hands, and His feet on earth. I called the previous chapter "Spiritually Out Of Shape" before the content was ever written. It seemed so fitting and I had no idea why, only to find out I was actually the one who was spiritually out of shape. *You see how God works?* I finally recognized the weight of my life on the earth. I never knew I had something so valuable on the inside of me to share with all of you. I now know who I am. I am who God said I am. I will boast in the Lord. There was a lot that I had to sacrifice to get to this point. It wasn't an easy journey but it was worth it. It was a struggle but He was always my strength. I am now prideful in the Lord. I am not exempt from the blessings and definitely not the struggles.

1 Peter 5:10-11 reads,

> *"But the God of all grace, who hath called us unto His eternal glory by Christ Jesus, after that ye have suffered a while, make you perfect, stablish, strengthen, settle you. To him be glory and dominion for ever and ever. Amen."*

I was enslaved to something I wanted to keep in the dark but darkness is where the enemy thrives. The moment the devil is exposed, he loses all of his power. Cast your cares before the Lord and allow Him to show you who you really are. He will begin to speak life over you and show you things about yourself, and your life, that you couldn't imagine. You must be open to receiving them. The Lord will always give you a choice.

I now understand what I have with the Holy Spirit. I had an assignment on my life and so do you. You have a right to boast in the name of the Lord when you understand what you are walking in and who He called you to be. Your life has weight to it too and the earth needs what God has put in you.

God gave me a key and stood me in front of a door. It was open all along and never needed to be unlocked. I had to pass the test before I could walk through. The key I was holding was never mine. It was the key someone else needed in order to find out who they are in God and unlock the door in their life. You are holding that key right now. *Do you have what it takes to find out what is on the inside of you? Do you have what it takes to find out who God has called you to be?* There are things we are all called to do that are assigned to someone's awakening but we need to ask God the right questions. Because I answered God's call, someone else can walk in the fullness of their life. The way God touches people is through people. All of our lives are attached to a key to unlock something for someone else. Our assignment may be the very thing that allows someone else to unlock their destiny. Spiritually, we all have a helper which is the help of the Holy Spirit. Physically, we are all called to be helpers of one another.

Whatever life throws at you, understand God is always with you. In the midst of your storm you may feel as if the wind is controlling you but remember it is God who is controlling the wind. When faced with your wilderness, remember, that it will happen, that it had to happen and you will be glad it happened.

www.ingramcontent.com/pod-product-compliance
Lightning Source LLC
Chambersburg PA
CBHW050917160426
43194CB00011B/2439